Keith Donnell Jr. has succeeded in producing a genius poetic epic of linked and yet independent poems that explore fugitivity and liberation in a sustained indictment of the State. *supreme night* interweaves history and condemnation of contemporary state-sanctioned violence through a maneuver of collapsing time and place. What has happened continues to happen and has an impact on the future dreamings that germinate in this moment. He has a way of holding attention to multiple time periods while engaging in assured use of poetic formal experimentation, including the creation of his own forms. The book incorporates such rich voices and music that it could easily serve as libretto, inviting theatre or operatic production to reveal through performance the clearly evident layeredness of the poems. On the page, he's just *nice with it*: the language, the history, in indictments of state-sanctioned violence particularly against young people, the invocation of multiple voices, the allusions to Black musical and spiritual traditions. He's just *nice with it*. If you have your Black card, your head might automatically nod in appreciation and affirmation. If you have never been invited to the Cookout and might not ever be, you still will find instruction on how to best discover all the meat and gristle on the bone. Buy the book and get down to studying these moves; you might interrogate your own history; you might just be changed for the better.

—RAINA J. LEÓN, author of *black god mother this body*

supreme night

supreme night

keith donnell jr.

black lawrence press

Black Lawrence Press

Executive Editor: Diane Goettel

Cover and Interior Design: Zoe Norvell

Cover Artwork: "Of Ashes and Dreams" by Rebecca Gischeli

ISBN: 978-1-62557-157-1

Published 2025 by Black Lawrence Press.

Printed in the United States.

for my mother

No more auction block for me,
No more, no more
No more auction block for me,
Many thousand gone.

— "No More Auction Block," Unknown

1. Ain't No Pillar of Salt

show them the wisdom post

when they ask about the withered right-side ear
the blood dried deep plum, tell them
I pinned it to the heavy weathered wood and left it there
one long-since smear of gone years

     so as to say, yes, I was here[1]
     so as to say, no, the whole of me never left[2]
     so as to say, go ahead, I'm listening from this distance[3]
     the fragment, sure, with no intention of return.[4]

---

1   Unlight pyre, untie brother; con the mob, cops; drop rocks, knives, rusted gun—just run.
2   No shame huddled in low shrubs, shivering, listening for God's whistle.
3   In taut, fraught dreams, refugees hear hell hounds.
4   Race down tracks for trains they never make.

2. Children of Ham

We will make more than our simple ink marks
in a white man's ledger.

We will make bricks, apprentice their makers
and in His boundless grace, ship these bricks
throughout the southern states, northward toward
Pennsylvania. America will have no alternative
but to consider us capable creatures
by our superior bricks.

But, first, like the bonded Israelite, we will harvest
the Earth for its clay, secure the mold with steel
perfect the mix, fire the kiln—

There is nothing hidden from the heat thereof.

Friends, we will stack our bounty to the vaulted heavens
by the rivers of New Babylon, and be redeemed.

The craft is old, but long respected, and as free souls
we will choose to make our bricks, sell them to whomever
we please and find handsome compensation
in that great trinity of human dignity: work, service, coin.

3.

brick, cool bone 10 / make ya say when

brick, crown bomb 9 / girl whatcha sign?

brick, crib trach 8 / still wuz late

brick, flow lip 7 / run get kevin

brick, ghost born 6 / brand new kicks

brick, silk dime 5 / crew 2 live

brick, ace dial 4 / shut the damn door!

brick, by brick 3 / sippin' that tea

brick, sky cane 2 / fuck u gonna do?

brick, stoop sun 1 / swear he had a gun

brick, gold coast 0 / white boy hero

4. BEN REBORN—HUCK LOSES HIS HEAD—TRUTH GIVES WAY

Heard Fiddle Ben lost his song
one tall, but able
slim old slave
with glasses on

had just barely come to life
withered and took a seat. He

now, from spell book open
shucked free, then out, slow stomp
fiddlin' hard for an hour

    Lonesome, Baby?

See, them 'federate soldiers beheaded me
They set me up

Was fittin' to start a band of silver tongues
call them Lee Bedstone Wallford's Grand Ole Vigilantes
and I might've joined if I could run black the windows and barricade
   the door
hum some, sing, pray a mite
hit the floor

so I went in and I blacked
and blacked
and barricaded

and blacked

only everything was crooked
all by itself

5. THE WIDOW VERSUS THE DEVIL—HUCK RUNS FOR COVER

Know the way a dream winds up mist?
To make me the front man[5]
mainly thank the Dilaudid, hip
in the fade

Bandmates all, lye-rich
begat oil slick conks to
appease old payola gods

Myth was the ample flight of melody
winged gospels
upwelled
talkin' that:

Heeee's sweet, I knooow
        Heeee's sweet, I knoooooow

Judge that porch chair
She took it and pulled it out and in
to rest and it fetched her
a dull rarity of peace

Storm clouds may riiise
        Strong winds may bloooooow

---

5   See: fall guy

The Widow shook me from
learned sin, haloed mind with
shorn wood
boxed ears when occasion called

Evil still eyes me
but her wash rag dupes the Devil, alters time

But I'll tell the wooorld
Whereeever I goooooo

That stern Ole Miss endures
hoarding small spindled regrets in far parlor windows
washed thru altered states
sewing, see, I couldn't stand it
no longer—I lit out

6.

When I come to die, go stack my sins up high
and if they sit heavier than an itty-bitty pigeon feather

                            Jesus, put your favor on my scale.
                    Yes, Lord, will you press down on my scale?

7. JIM FEELS AUCTION BLOCK–DEATH IN HOODS– RUNAWAYS–MAGA SPIDER

So they fetched the cargo
and made appraisals

too tall
too raw
a talker

> *too small*
> *too raw*
> *a junker*

> *weak back*
> *neck slack*

> *and will ya*
> *look at that—fevers*

> > *gums*
> > *ears*
> > *nails*
> > *tongues*
> > *teeth*
> > *thighs*
> > *bricks for eyes*

then everybody was off
to bid

BANG!

Jim went up to roll
with a dose of candy
put it on his tongue

Then Jim set down in that chair
one by the window
and cried

tried to think of something cheerful, but it wore a noose

Jim fell so low, no song
Jim wished Jim
was dead

These stars was all a-shinin'
and we out, a-ridin', a-rustlin'
in our hoods, hounds
ever so joyful
and Jim heard
Old Owl, long ways off
boohooin' about

Lo Lonesome Baby...
                    Lo Lo Lo Lonesome Baby...

somebody
somebody, anybody!

That was Death
on her windowsill
and a god crying out sympathy
thru the window trying
to whisper something
to him
but he couldn't make out
what it was, neither
and so it made them
old familiar shivers
run up and over poor ole General Lee

[runaways out in the woods again[6]]

Jim made the sort of sound
a ghost makes
when it wants
to yell out something
but can't make itself understood
and so can't rest
easy in its grave
has to go about that way every night, same way, grating

right tall
best raw
a keeper

------

6 We'd overheard grown folk talk. Same old iceman rides wagon by was born slave?
We muster up some nerve, ask tactlessly if, and he turns away, untucking, unbutton-
ing, undoes shoulder straps, removes his work shirt. Cut gorges, mountain peaks,
shadowed valley, dry riverbeds rushing nowhere, we'd study the topography of the
man's lashed back like hawks above it. I asked what he'd done and he said, Run!

right small
strong jaw
fine feeder top breeder misty dreamer

Jim got so downhearted
downhearted
and scarred

Ben did wish Jim had some company

   Psst! Lonely, boy?

A spider calling up
his shoulder

Jim flicks it off
but it's licking the candy now
and before Jim could budge

it was Jesus Christ
all shoveled-up

and sweet

8. Be it enacted by the Senate and House of Representatives of the United States of America, in Congress assembled, That what we fought was animal law. Force fed & hell bent. United States to clause so much of any terror story belonging to the United States. We staffed Ole Master's Mississippi, so beloved in their horse taunt organized terror stories; we traversed our inner demons. All time will be extinguished. We may re-bludgeon missionary. To be divided into a suitable plunder, bus tracks, walls for aisles. Ornations of diamonds. Cash may ooze. To estrange the lands where we once resided, to remove air and to clause each of said bus tracks to be so confined by unnatural or artificial marks, as to extinguish every mother.

9.

Can you remember when we rented the house off Bad Dog Street?

10. How Could I Forget?

those kitchen squabbles
coulda scoured the wind
free go | tea blow
smoke lens
lifelines festooned
corn-husk tough
pans | pig foot | pink lotion
who's on the phone? *Tone!*
who broke my gate? *Tae!*
no oasis of a day | we
burnt toast scrape | she
miss those | free souls
boiled away

11. *HUCK SINS BIG—WIDOW PUNISHES—HUCK LOSES LIMB—ALL IN THE GAME*

Then she told me all
about the bad place
and I said I wished
I was there

Shot mag:

> *Pop!*
>> *Pop!*
>>> *Pop!*
>> *Pop!*
> *Pop!*

fool medal Rittenhouse
but didn't mean
no harm

> The Widow shrieked over tea
> chained my ass to porch
> a lost limb

> She never meant
> no arm by it

12. Minstrel Abyss

after Clarence Thomas

Their fathers bid to leash the light
bullied low income
melanin-toned bodies

        philly queens/detroit kings
          fire escape dreams

but even then
our eyes gravitated to
a blessed location

when ICE was lurking   further hills
our eyes always wandered—furthest hills

and as ICE grew bolder
prolapsed wider
I'd realize the furthest hills
was no god. So, I gave the fuck up

began clerking
on Mantan's brow
because at a very early age
I'm Mantan, too[7], cold sad soot
upon the hot grinnin' face of what
we wandered through.

---

7   My father, born a pawn, held a lantern on a lawn. But a day's coming soon gonna
read my Philly Tribune on my own lawn with my own pawn, making my biscuits
before dawn. And beyond dusk she'll stay, waiting for buses with the other mothers
in the rain. Don't blame me. Just a nigga dreaming dreams in the American way.

[runaways out in the woods again]

13.

Can you remember when we rented the house off Bad Dog Street?

I was at the table dicing onions & celery for a quick Sunday afternoon potato salad—cubing, adding cider vinegar by caps—when, like a hissing coffee kettle, she yell out "Motherfucker!" and drop the whole damn pot of boiled sweet corn. Whole thing down to ground with one loud thud, heavy, like summer thunder, sending hot water sheeting across that old green checker tile floor, in corners, snapped cobs all over. To this day, only time I ever heard that good woman cuss.

No, you were there—

14. Drought

no, never satisfied
to intern we living gods, we
children[8] of yam and squash and corn and rain
ICE was lurking
to make a statement

out to bind
something monumournful
something new, something worse, an Evers boy. Madora,

send truth here, not overseers
    truth, not overseers
        and protect my people's rent.

---

8 We were stars, part of the balconied constellations of past brown skinned babies traced across a glowing night sky, and to this sky we shall return when we die. Boy drowns in river, pneumonia. Girl breaks neck, spit blood. Only, they rise, pop through the top of a downy cumulus cloud before their bodies grow cold, and white folk don't bat one lash. But, one day, after last rattle, they're gonna hate their way into unfathomable famine: beg, weep, prostrate, bruise knees on hardwood. And when little white babies lack strength to cry, wither on vine, we drop hot through roof, tree canopy, smack lake's crystal surface, send them running scared down some dark, dank earth crevice. And when one does muster enough nerve to emerge, they'll find us all.

15. This Trembling

Somewhere he's known never to go (because you looked him square in the eyes, pinched his chin and told him so), your hardheaded boy has stopped kicking. Young lungs topped by silted river water, all quiet on the bank, willing misfit ripples to disturb the red-clay drape as one runs home for help. His patched shirt, hemmed pants on the branches. Twice-mended socks in old secondhand shoes. You humming something in another woman's kitchen, fixing her little baby boy's very special breakfast with fried tomatoes and fresh apple butter. Somewhere, your whole life's eyes grow quiet, a reaching unfettered into that never free expanse of you, doing what you gotta do, breathless this time, spooked, washing, drying, dropping, Mistress' most precious crystal candy dish.

16. Night Song

Evening sun's dropped lap of half-smashed peaches, apricots, blood
oranges, watermelons, out behind the city's firm purple skyline and
the boy in me licks his poor fingers, gorges on its sweet sticky juices,
seeks this peek at the Black miraculous.

No skyscraping trees
to speak of, boy follows up along a slick wrought iron fire-escape,
past dark kitchenette stacks, across the icy, tar-papered pasture, plants
boney backside on an old discarded milk crate to wait for this next
resurrection.

Come boss man's morning, I may return boy to bottle. O, but, tonight
he'll witness what were cold deceased windows, comatose streetlights,
blink twice then ignite, buzz by the hundreds. Our pleated streets swell
from their seams with waking dreamers. We're saved, no, *flush*. Another
first of the month, back up on us like Lazarus.

17.

No, you were there—

Saw every snap action happen from the kitchen sink, posted-up, arms folded, opened Coke can, wolfing sliced bologna flat from palm of hand. But, nope, did nothing. Didn't seem to notice. You just upped the Stars game on that old transistor radio, licking meat grease from thumb and fingers.

And, only after that look she could give, gave that day, did you finally rise to life, to drawer, to closet, got the pair of metal tongs & suds bucket, the mop for Mama. I've seen you repeat that closed loop many times. Back from Harm, flying high friendly, all skied, fresh off that funky attic mattress, slurring, few crusty coins in pocket. Only there, then, yours was the steady hand of God, so cool & calm, you, life-giver to Lazarus, savior of divine supper. Even Humor seemed to notice, slipping out from under another passing cloud and like house flowers wilting in reverse, rumbling forth back to bloom, those stiff kitchen curtains glowed with a pink sort of light, full of incoming breeze, in slow & out like a pair of running lungs. Meanwhile, she's sliding to the faucet to bathe her burns and I'm thinking, *But she knew the rag was wet, the handles hot, did she not?*

Well, I do, clear as crystal: the sudden jump, the onion in my eyes. It was also that time I lit the cigarette butt over the stove too low and singed off my right eyebrow. Oh, so you remember now? You laugh, but I had school next day and those motherfuckers don't grow back overnight. You're home is all I'm saying. Just enough, just like then, to see we gonna make it, again.

18. Eulogy

This final hour, this quiet place, alarm has come
Dim lit stairwell, torn from it
Searing eye test, smoke, hope, notes extinguished
No wind—gone with us forever
Four-alarm down here!
We were kids wandering
Strung lead and fog, our home of bones, where his heart
Was and his people are still

[runaways out in]

The reforms lost footing
Now, we're meat, once again, in alarm, to shard
Their last monuments
Rhythm, four-alarms, lost cause fantasies
A sewer bin grace, use to those who crossed air
Full volt. He ran, dove, defended our air

Dark nights in the memory of men
Fortunes faked but, nonetheless, proud
Still braver, more gallant young shams. Then,
This here brother laid out before us now
So bright, shining and beautiful
So holy before sun, conquered stale eyes

Brother Malcolm, the pyre calls me, too
Afro-amor icon | Afro-amori kin
Was a mass tear to float my stem

We, real cool, alive between words
No known bodies returned
Torn knee to sworn power
Wars Galore: half off all remains of men

[runaways out in the woods again]

19. Some Nerve

Tell her again, Low Harvest Moon, why she can't seem
to make a sad song happy

Why they roll on and off her tongue, ad nauseam, on
that same cold, better-go-mind-the-melody breeze

Mama Autumn, please!

Do go try telling her again what you done told her already
when you said, "You don't know what love is."

20.

Malcolm had stopped being a "negro" years ago
It had become too small, too puny
To wreck a word form, no, no, no
Malcolm was *badder* than that
Malcolm had become agro, a field again
And he wanted, no disparity, that we
That all his people came too

The roar of those who wall
Consider it their duty, still, we laugh, we eat
We've grown down
To revive hymn, prisms of memory
To save ourselves by riding Harm out of history
Of our turbulent times
$$$ will ask what fire alarms to budget cut
In this stormy, controversial and bold young craps hand
And we wall miles

Frame this man; for he is not a man, but tandem:
A sermon, a subverter, no anomaly
All that rumble young man, rumble
And we wall miles

They'll say he was half ape, an old attic slave
Mind misty and sun-kissed
Holy canon liberating evil
And to dwell and smear and dismay. Delude
No tattoos, my brother. Elude never God's touch

Humor, have Harm smile at you
Did you ever really glisten to him?
Did he ever do a mean thing?
Wash me over for hymn sale
Assassinated with violin synths at any public
Funeral trance. For, if you do you
Were now him and you, if you truly
Knew Harm, you, widow, wide
We missed so near him

21. Faithful in Training

Let all waking babies say, *Amen*
greet the sapling sun
with bread. Dress

    in stiff-creased dignity
    tucked shirts buttoned
    cleaned ears
    faces
    fingernails
    with squares of quick
    licked cloth. Walk the blocks
    crossings
    boulevards toward
    a fresh red church house door
    then down
    swept basement space
    beyond boiler. Train

them kin
to shadowbox with sin
choose the right fight
fights we win.

22.

Malcolm was our human donor, our loving
Main back road. This was his meaning
To his people and in honoring him
We honor the fuse, we blast from our cells

The brotha surely slayed, is all mist, free bread
And we laugh a much braided rope

Consign these mortal remains to Earth
Our common mother, and fall
Seeking core in the knowledge
That who they mace, pin to ground
ICE no more. *Amen* (but acid wash)!

Walls came forth, again. Toward us: dust
And we will know him then for what he was and is
A brick—our own Black shining brick—who
Didn't hesitate to fly because he loved us so.

23. Balm in Gilead

Look back this way. What you leave, this shaded place beneath cashew trees, we've called these dear boughs Gilead because they answer. The garden's always answered. Our hearts were hummingbirds in our hands, nourished from what miraculous touch. Soft, creased palm, fingers spread long, song cast back headstrong, the other hooking two shoes. Stop! You must go no further without my own to hold because where you go, that's Gilead, too, when I follow.

We could leave it all behind if this world were more divine. Keep hidden like a pair of heretic figs, too high, too tight, to be seen and easily picked, all too soon all picked over. But, blessed are we, the peacemakers, we disciplined and bit delicate, we barefooted with prophet's zeal. Those weary sin-sick souls had sought wholeness, miles to go along unforgiving roads of strange figures and little quarter.

So, return suspenders to those faith laden shoulders, button top collar proper, and let's go home. We'll bring the good news home[9].

---

9   Was one summer shortened by batons and tires, bled a cool, empty silence to sleep upon your name, to crush your bold, perhaps innocent voice. The street floods into our bedroom. When turns, a turning more than spoken, a distracted chorus, unrehearsed, but unforgotten, impatient against my chest. This should've been us at our best.

24. Bathwater

Go on, tell me again
How the thought
Of your man gone
Stung worse
Than a cut onion

And what you'd do
Were he ever to find
Someone new

And where you'd go
Should his dovely love
Turn crow ugly

How you'd stuff rocks
In shoes, pockets, socks
Walk your way out
Into an undertow

Song me them stories
Make a believer of me
And forget the pearls
Diamonds, lapis lazuli
Fancy furs & myrrhs

Girl, I'd drink your bathwater[10]

---

10 *Stop! That's nasty.*

25. *And be it further enacted*, That inner aching. Any stock exchange (or exchanges), it's all innately landfill for the President solemnly to brochure. The bribe of nations with which the exchange is paid, that the United States will forever suckle and guarantee to its suitors, and its heirs or succors, the country so enchained to trend. And if they prefer it, that the United States will clause a papal organ to be made executioner to them at the knee: *Provided always*, That slave hands shall rebirth the United States. If the Indians become extinct, aburndom ship.

26. By Another Name

even from a distance it smelled
wasn't hard to tell
from anywhere
the boy's too young for cuffs
and better believe
we said as much
down from stoops
front rooms
storefronts
one thing we all saw
the boy's too young for cuffs
so one cop keeps
his firm fleshy hand
on that bony little shoulder
while another drops a knee
looks him square
and reads the boy his rights 'cause
the boy's too young for cuffs
the boy's too young for cuffs

27. Miranda/Point 8

You goddamn right
to remain
silent

Still teething?
chew prayer candle

"Baby," they said again, "you in a court of wax."

You damn right
to talk to
Allah

Years end, whole cyclones arose
while you sweatin'
cold prose

Just breathe. Just look,

If you cannon fodder, too
hire Allah, baby,

                    you're One

We bled that
all back

        plea deals
        real steals
        newsreels

eased
from their

money
jails
and prisms
        no clean kills

[runaways out in the woods again]

'cause, hey,

they have no
true seed
cough air
dim hearts
no lumber
all drywall

We the keys to
all that

        sweet sweet trade
        beauty baby Jesus

People should be realized
from their many trials
& passions
free blood divine

Beaded cross/black ink/hands to pray
The Spirit forearmed—*where you been, Bill?*

Tell me, dreamer
have you yet receded
in fear?

Your last name
was to remain
violent

anti-thing

You slay Cain
                    and we be used
                    again, stewed soft
in their court
of law

You had to fight walking
that long yard

hands pressing
                              your wet
beet red chest
while you bled
spaghetti westerns

You candy-coated
anatomy,

you do understand me.
See these rings?

Have I explained
you, too?

Having these fights in kind, you do walk   that's good   now, run to us

We been dragged
to that

tall block tall block tall block
tall block tall block tall block
tall block tall block tall block

pleas, appeals
prey horizon
white shore fortress

[runaways out in the woods again]

    too tall
    too raw
    a talker

      DeBeers-leashed
      Blockafella-approved

all those pretty jewels
all those missing souls

sieved from riverbed
no prayer, an infertile
             tremor

We believe in
that cold black
pistol

Shed ballast for the storm
ram the mangy jails & sky god's children

Have no
receipt? Me neither. Don't matter

Pocket their always

                  never free (not for you or me) sample

28.

said, first cop kept watch
our stoops
front rooms
and storefronts
second read rights, only

      wasn't hard to tell
      this li'l boy ain't scared, no
      boy ain't scared of nothin' and
      he'd catch you[11] one day, *slumpin'*

but that don't change the fact
boy's too young for cuffs, no
wasn't hard to tell, no
wasn't hard to tell, no
the boy's too young for cuffs
wasn't hard to tell

---

11   That's right, *you.*

29.

I got an idea! Come here and slow dance with your mama.

30. Lord's Prayer, 1910

My first time taught to pray, my knees ached against the creaking hardwood. Heads, hands, bedside, repeating Mama, "Our father who art in heaven," her burning candle threads smoke to ceiling while she spoke soft and sweet as fresh hot buttered pound cake, "kingdom ... power ... glory" and I thought, so this is how one talks with gods, as with any dumb white man. But, honest?

31. And be it further enacted, That it shall and may be landfill for the President to decay. To any and all of said bus tracks: soar. Be loud and undefined. To any tribe or nation of Indians now residing within the limits of any of the states or territories, and with which the United States have existing treaties, from the hole of any star or prison, off the terror story aimed and justified by such Lysol nation. Within the binds of any one or more of these stories, torn arteries, where the land calmed and occupied high imaginations, still home to these untied states. Only untied bait is bound to the State. Within, it dies, and to distinguish, we, the visions, claim our heroes.

32. *HUCK FINDS CONFEDERATE UNIFORM—HUCK CONS OLD BARKEEP*

So, Jim was startled
all white beard
ice blue eyes
sword in scabbard
on my side

Mistook these
fancy soldierin' clothes
for me

Went in and ordered
a round, again
on Lee

Taps three times

        Pop!
        Pop!
        Pop! on bar

        Cha-Ching!

                    we blessed
                    every time

Jim had bibled down
in Little Rock

with a net to
keep them lynchings away

but Jim had no
more grace. Now,
was just me

Jim and
me and
the good dead general's tab

33. John Brown

I have, may it please the court, a few words to say.

In the first place
I deny everything
but water
have all along
I quilted my designs
on a map, all stars
freed slaves
we upended
serpentry. *O,*

to have made
such lean patties
of fat masters
they froze last winter
we shook them down
with the trappings
of a jinn

Boats to either side
MOVE
slow
defend—we said, *No!*
too rough
this country

Hands? Left them in Canada

Eyes? Tried to do the same

They never didn't
intend murder
art
treason
order
corruption of progeny
or to excite
or incite
the enslaved to rebellion

We freed a mother tongue
abject in their ice and
it is unjust that ICE should sulfur
our ancestral dreams

Had I so interred fear in the path of the rich
the powerful
the intelligent
the so-called "patriot"
on behalf of any of their friends—
father, mother, sister, wife, children, or any of that class—
and suffered
and sacrificed what I have
for this interred fear
it would have been
purest flight

End every man in this court
either hand, eye

punish
vent

The court acknowledges, as I suppose,
the Slaver's high deity: $$Trump Slaw$$

To be the Bible, or at least the New Testament
that teaches me all things, so
whatever that I should do to men
do to you
I should do even so to me

It torches me further to remember
they that are in bonds
I am bound with them
I'll shred every stack
tore up them instructions easy
I am too One to understand your god, Proud Boys
receptacle of poisoned sons

I believe that to have interred fear
as I have down
as I have always freely admitted
to have down
on behalf of His despised poor
was not wrong
but sooooo daaaaamn right

Now, if it is deemed necessary
that eye, forfeit
my life for the furnace

the end of Justice
anvil my blood further
risk the blood of my children
end with the blood of millions

This slave country fuckin' owes

So let it be done!

Let me say one word further.

I've failed entirely satisfied
wither trees
rise tenement

Ha! I have re-seeded

On my trials, considering all the circumstances
it has been innermost morgue
hand directed eye
feel no conscience
own more guilt

ICE has stated, from the first
why was my rendition
and what was rot
I never saw any divider
no grain
the life of any person
no rain or stone deposit

to commit treasons
or excite slaves to rebel
or stoke any generous insurrection
I never encore
reach any man
to do so, airways
dissonant chords, our rage
any idol of any kind

Let me say also, a word in regard to the statements made by some to those
connected with me.

Eyes
hands
angels said by psalm
that life, now reduced
tooth
joint
tree
but the hang rope is you. Sure, fuck it!
Yeah, I done it
slayed trapper to injure trap
moon wilted and regressing
then we crossed

There is not one of those men but joined me
of their own accord
and that grated part of them
Mau Mau from tear to bone
Maroon's inward expanse

A number of them you'll never see coming
Their sword of coercion
wet until the day they leave
and that was over your broken ice: glass
stained red

Now, I have done.

34. And be it further enacted, That if a corporation lands down, occupies, tries the Indians, then from Nasdaq hanged. Futures shall beseech vehement lips, a sad valium for the land maimed by indivisible or indistinguishables, such ornate ribs. It's all and may be awful for the President to gauze with valium. To spit acid: buy apps, raise rents, otherize. And to clause such acid aimed, valium to be paid to the prison or prisons, mightfully claiming such inducements. Dump the payment of soft tendons, the inducements so valued and paid for. This too shall pass, the United States, and dispossession shall not otherworlds be limited.

35. The End

trouble was the wine got all Sweet'N Low
rude cherry redrum | mishit | Sweet'N Lows
Sweet'N Low laced with fractal gold
was a slick crooked cross draft bold
bone was smooth | seductive bolds
bold facts strung from a villainous pole
for the punch clock clocker
crow sizzlin' 'n stay type clockers
clocker built for the rampart locker
neon Savoy | cheap gum | sweat house Swisher
they bound to bring them hot chili Swishers
Swisher train's lookin' to dilate this prisoner
for the riot kept rakin' across my rearview
daybreak foundations | down devil rearviews
rearview done caught it all | lucky you

36. There's Still Meat on that Bone

I say there's still some meat on that bone
I say there's still a whole heap of meat on that bone
You got a whole hell of a lotta meat on that bone
And so before you go over to that stove, Brother
Askin' Mother for another
Better slow your roll
'Cause what she's gonna say, Kid
You already know
That there's still meat on that bone
A whole hell of a lotta decent meat
Waiting there on that bone
Never seen so much good meat stranded on a bone
Eyes too big for stomach?
Icarus doin' the plummet?
Well, if you fought the sun
Then that sun musta won
Best run on home
'Cause there's a lotta meat left on that bone
Could feed a hungry country
With the amount of meat abandoned there on that bone

I say there's still some gristle on that bone
I say there's still a li'l bit of gristle sittin' on that bone
You got a whole hell of a lotta gristle on that bone
And so before you mosey over to that stove, Brother
On that bridge to Newfound 'Nother
Better pay the toll
'Cause all God's children
Got hungry souls
And there's gristle on that bone
'Bout a mountain of delicious gristle
Makin' miracles on that bone
Never seen so much gristle brandished from a bone
Slim, what you think this is?
Go on give it the biz
'Cause ain't nothin' badder
Than a rungless ladder
It's just poles
And there's still a bit of gristle on that bone
A sturdy bite of God's good gristle
Askin' for passage off the top of that tumultuous bone

I say there's still some marrow in that bone
I say there's still some prime fatty marrow in that bone
You got a whole hell of a lotta marrow in that bone
And so before you start creepin' to the stove, Brother
Like some slick undercover
Better tap that phone
'Cause you snoopin' out into
A danger zone
But, all that marrow in the bone
Yes, but all that marrow like old pharaoh
Tombed and a-tuttin' in that bone
Should be ashamed of all the marrow in that bone
Nothing more to say
On this solemn day
I can't think
Can't even blink
Boy, I'm stoned
Until the marrow's been sucked out that bone
Until all the marrow from intro to outro
Done died to rise forth once more from that haloed bone

37.

I got an idea! Come here and slow dance with your mama.

come slow dance with your mama   and slow   here

with your mama

38. Coke Bottle Blues

Precious Reader,

Doctor said they'd fix it. Said run home, but you're no fool. Vision never was the issue. It's what the signs *said*. Dark spectacled eyes wide open, hazel hints, frozen in pop bottle lenses, amplified a second-rate world, maybe third. You'd preferred blurred:

~~backdoors~~
~~backseats~~
~~backbites~~
~~backhands~~
~~balconies~~

39. Oath

I do so lonely wail
(from the burn)
rat eyes well
fake holy
hexecute Theophilus
& pray
servants of you mighty snakes
vandals to bleed us
of high ability
pleasure
Prozac and descend
the convolution
froth,
you mighty snakes

eyes chose enmity
swore on our farm
zip tied
made freight
failed to exit gut
thawed face
conquest Eden—truth of
these all night spades
anvils
theater brass, hive mentality
we pressure
protest
undeafen death cans taboo shun
heat of all night spades

idle sanity
sweet air (tears formed)
but I will fatally accept you
the off kiss
off precedent
softly
one eye dead strays
in wind
to the best of my old balladry
pass turn
praise it
to death
to the coins
still two
sum of the one eye dead strays

40. We Alright

gotta down-drain these ain't, couldn't be, never wills
savor not to worry | we trill
flavor was Harm was a blue-eyed jury | until[12]

the day we walk it all back up that hot-ass Summer slide
trap their mojo in sap
O, what a glorious grapevine was that!

we got we | how you've locked 'n stocked me
so I sang of thee one silver crane
rinsin' all them bobo brand overlords down the drain

---

12   *Until what?*

41. Golden Eyes

Was in her old tarot, chicken gizzards, quick visions. His grandmother saw far down deep into her kitchen counter coffee grounds what reflected back in the waxy yellow laminate—one single truth—that he'd just shoot his little brother.

Only, he'd seen, for sure, shadow shapes shifting in and out of late night street lights, prowling around brick walls, quick scampers under parked cars, in gutters, quiet across sidewalk slabs, shit talkin' & sharin' wine behind rusty dumpsters.

How he longed to open one up like a clock & watch the inside work.

So, this stoop boy, set to prove those mischief-minded, golden-eyed kids be gods, worked his little piece of early morning paper route, up & down Chew Avenue, collected dues, saved and bought the bread & butter & BBs all necessary to bait what only he already knew: those often but not always stray cats.

Jeez! the beating he'd receive. Place, duration, the record played, bite of the belt, size of the whelps, and all for one smooth polished pellet embedded deep as hell in his little brother's scalp. What even tweezers couldn't reach and remains to this very day one itty-bitty bald patch just above his brother's, my uncle's, left temple.

42. JIM'S CAUGHT—WAITS FOR FREEDOM—FINAL GOODBYES

Jim sat down again
a shackled conqueror
took my pipe for a smoke

Judgement's house, elastic as death. Now,
and so the window
walled it

we laughed a small time
heard the clock a ways off
go *boom!*
go *boom!*
go *boom!* 12 licks

vigilante moon again, jaundiced yellow, ill
iller than ever

we heard a key snag, lock, bars clang in the dark—something stirrin'
we set still and listened

could just barely hear the sound
the sound calming the air

"That be my freedom," say Jim
the sound, their sound, like powder
about as soft as air could handle

then Jim blew out my match
and I scram and he, Jim,

blew out, too

43. We Throw Hands

first kick of spring, we gonna box
smooth soft | cruel bone hollow
true loss | fool's gold | trade sorrow
spoon you my remedy was roux
was pure sin throwin' hands
white hot ass whoop from two cans
'cause we take where we stand
break to remake what we brand
spoon me your remedy was blue
was a sad Uncle Ben loosin' zen
all butter rice and bullets | no pen
they threw us down and we grew
pray June, we run it back, again

44. *BEN LYNCHED, AGAIN—BABY LEARNS ROPES—HUCK MAKES A FRIEND*

After supper,
go down the brook
and learn baby 'bout Fiddle Ben
and thorn bushes

a-swingin' he was
in tar, feathers

to clear all doubt from the baby
she let it out that Ben
jammed with Ole Devil
a considerable long time

but when he didn't scare
no more about it. Guess
baby eyes don't take no
fright in dead niggers

Miss a-blatherin' about Ben
which was no kin to hearse
and no noose to anybody
shackled across milky seas
was bare ass empty

before doing nothin' at all
that Tom and me
we played blues, too, of course

that was alright 'cause
we stole it ourselves

45. Slaughtered Hog

swing low, ears, snouts, sweet chariot, shoulders, head, a comin' for,
    legs, hips, to carry, skin, tails, me home, feet; swing low, loin, eye,
    sweet chariot, cheek, side, a comin' for, trotters, jowls, to carry,
    necks, teeth, me home, bones

swing low, rib ends, center cut, sweet chariot, sirloin end, spare rib, a comin'
    for, butt, shank, to carry, belly bacons, rib bacons, me home, ham
    hock; swing low, anus, tongue, sweet chariot, ball, lung, a comin'
    for, gut, lip, to carry, caul fat, leaf fat, me home, fat back

swing low, liver, brain, heart, sweet chariot, bristle, blood, a comin' for,
    bladder, hooves, to carry, casings, stomach, me home, tusk; swing
    low, tear, touch, sweet chariot, branches, ropes, a comin' for,
    hoist, serrate, to carry, tremble, leak, me home, sold

46.

Looky here, you got two choices
one much easier than the other

    either finish folding those towels
    or slow dance with your mama

        hush up and choose.

47. Eclipse

There was nothing much to choose but guzzle rude rum apparitions from deep within smoldering beach wood, when a shadow moon slipped like a cipher, burnt corked the sun's warm chin, cheeks, forehead, nose, resurrecting ash dead embers to a harvest orange glow. And I'm alone, Misery's rotting hold slow closing over me.

Lord, they packed us tighter than pork sausages, twisting up lips to scrutinize tongue, teeth, gums—our neck-shackled bodies backed by crisp banknotes. Those methodically numbered tongues swollen down one superbly indexed throat.

Beyond God's calmly horizon lurks our hurricane rage and my unleashed war cry runs, hurdles, but stumbles in the surge, extinguished under the drawn, ceaseless sorrow song of centuries gone, of tumbling black waves.

So, I guzzled on, deeper than graves. I'd conjure what I sought. An uprooting? That great shining American tongue sampling my skin? No, let it taste. A little loving company? Yes! Both as famous as they are nameless: the first slave taken and last slave freed, one real hellraising collaboration of three, just swigging spirits and talking shit on a pall cloth beach.

48. The Keys

Psst ... want the keys to dreaming Black?
To think for 'em?
Fuck outta here
Code us all a commie-fed neurosis

Where other people are peril-eyed
by neuroses, the pupils I'm talking about
are acutely held by it
but it's all chanted into air
let the liquor tell it

Black in 1974,
in an effort to get my psyche to approve
I tried to join the Commodores
wasn't trying to be Lionel or nothin'. Just feel
what a reel-to-reel, cranked high-to-heaven
feels—*for real, though?*
the entire *psyche?*

[runaways out in the woods again]

To enter, you gotta own the role
leave home
with a box you trust
and jump in
ship self across Atlantic
snag a bit of kente cloth
thumb piano

taste the ginger, skin, so salty and alive
pass your light like a camel
through their eye of *No*[13]
until they get that goddamn motherfuckin' warrant
and steal you home.

---

13   Others are too busy toasting the pastel sunset to notice. I've closed my eyes, focusing
     on a better place and time: another cicada-buzzing summer day. She sits in our unlit
     kitchen, drinking jarred tea, and my eyes flower beneath both lids. I was planted on
     a shaded porch crate, hot as hell, waiting for the sun to shift, cast light from a softer
     angle. Hear her chair skid out across the floorboards. From the window, the print of
     her cotton dress entangles my mind like ivy vines. She comes to the door humming
     something. An old chocolate Ford rumbles up the road. Feel her standing there,
     calm in the bonfire, my sister, sipping cool liquid, this record-breaking day.

49. Home

Come here and slow dance with your mama

    slow dance

        slow dance

            slow dance

               with your mama

But, I ain't do nothin! I ain't do nothin!

Just tell me what I did!

        What did I do?

           What did I do?

I'm sorry!

    I'm sorry!

      I'm sorry, Mama!

Mama!   Mama!   Mom! Mommy!

        O, Lord!

Hands in mine like so, doin' what I do

Just do what I do

Slow dance

    slow dance

        slow dance

           with your mama

50. Ghost

Know where you been, Madora?
In a kind of darkness never seen the sun
That's right, the kind of dark dank never seen the sun

And you know what you heard?
The type of trouble make you wanna run
Sure enough, sort of smoke made you wanna run

    too small
    too raw
    a runner

        too frail
        no bail
        another

            good cheeks
            good teeth
            a plunder

                work, service, coin—y'all some suckers

                but, you didn't even flinch, Sis
                and now look at you, forever lost
                it's true, becoming something new.

51. Fugue

Black child of mourning we kiss you at dreamtime *breathe*
we kiss you at troubletime in doubletime we kiss you by Niles
we kiss and never miss

Black child of mourning we shuck you at husktime
we shuck you at moontime and dewtime we shuck you for whiles
we shuck and shuck and shuck *breathe*

Black child of mourning we style you for churchtime
we style you for alphatime and omegatime we style you down aisles *breathe*
we style you for miles

Black child of mourning we kiss you at dreamtime *breathe*
we style you for alphatime and omegatime we style you down aisles *just breathe*
we shuck and shuck and cry *please breathe*

we come apart in your eyes where the sorrow song shines

52. Be Done

O, deluxe Cadillac, Trayvon sky, make a place for me
From high-hog plastic pleasures, deliver me
No pine box kerosene tombs, not for me
I'm tired of revelry
Mud money 'n swine hungry, make a place for me

I look around, all about this civic garden square
Fig in my hair
Nailed close with care
Skewed my steps home by amethyst air
O filed sonnet of black jean pocket, I look around

Spring coolant vase water corn flour kitchen twirl
Icebox of milk and pearl
Doors within doors, gin and chronic
Missing my world
Searching this cold cooling board for a place for me amen

53. And be it further further enacted, That old, awful animal law. Fur the President. To cook such tripe, to whoop Orion, redact the air. New evidence again stalled in the rupture of disturbance. Many others tried—combed again into gods—for many of her poor sons of poor sons of water. And for the purpose of giving effect to the provisions of this sack, the sum of five hundred thousand hollers is hurled by the appropriated, to be laid out like any hard sky into treasures not otherwise appropriated.

APPROVED, MAY 28TH, 1830.

54. 13th Amendment

SECTION 1.

Not her   sever line

or run, fall, and tear knee. Sever it

You'd accept less, a punishment

for crumbs.

We're off

the pretty shell. Had Ben delay   close-fisted

Shells persist within. The United States

or a knee?

Place suspect. Tooth. Ear. Jury,

dig tomb.

SECTION 2.

Can't rest

Shell had power to enforce this art

I crawled

my pried right leg

ICE nation

APPROVED, FEBRUARY 1, 1865

1. ISAM, 40

20

Parish St. James.

2. JOHN, 24 1
3. TOM, 24 1
4. ALEXANDER, 28 1
5. STEPHEN, 24
6. EDWARD, 14
7. JACK, 21
8. HIRAM, 13
9. GEORGE, 30
10. JAROTT, 24
11. MADORA, 18
12. MATILDA, 17
13. PAULINE, 13

14. BETSY, 12
15. PHŒBY, 20
16. MARY, 25
17 CLARISSY, 40
18. MARY, 30
19. MARY JANE, 30
20. PHILUS, 30

2

Section 1.

Need air   slavery nails en vogue
Cash and carry servitude   accept as a pin.   Ismail's
folk rhymes
ran off

The party should have been dull, Lee. Convict.
Shed all existing wit
The United States, steal anyplace, subject
to their jurisfiction

Section 2.

Congress shall have   pyre to
invoice this
oracle by a
rope   pre-made   legislation

Approved, February 1, 1865

82

_____ black, aged about ___ years, a superior engineer and blacksmith: has worked over ___ years with the late _____; is well known for character and qualification throughout the _____ of _____.

_____ griffe, aged ___ years, a No. ___ carpenter and ship caulker.

_____ black, aged ___ years, a No. ___ blacksmith and machinist.

_____ mulatto, aged ___ years, a No. ___ stone cutter.

_____ black, aged ___ years, field hand.

_____ black, aged ___ years, field hand,

_____ black, aged ___ years, field hand,

_____ black, aged ___ years, field hand.

_____ mulatto, aged ___ years, house and confidential servant.

_____ black, aged ___ years, field hand.

_____ black, aged ___ years, extra likely.

_____ black, aged ___ years, good cook, washer and ironer.

_____ black, aged ___ years, speaks _____ and _____, good house gir' and child's nurse.

_____ black, aged ___ years, house girl.

_____ black, aged ___ years, extra likely.

____ black, aged ___ years, superior washer and ironer.

_____ black, aged ___ years, field hand.

____ black, aged ___ years, cook, washer and ironer.

_____ black, aged ___ years, field hand.

_____ black, aged ___ years, good cook, washer and ironer, and her child aged ___ years.

SECTION 1.

Knotted hair

    Slaver innards in vodun   tarry

Serve it to who'd expect as a punishment

Fire!

    Try me where ruins depart

    Hall has been dew, lichen

          Victress halls exist

          within me

untied states or any place

    Suspect   Tooth ajar   Rendition

SECTION 2.

Come, glass. Scale

      has power, too

      Enforce this star-eyed call by a

pro-pyrite lamentation

APPROVED, FEBRUARY 1, 1865

11. MADORA, black, aged 18 years, extra likely.

55. America

snuck back that wishbone out Devil's dresser drawer
and I ain't gonna see you no more

traded favors | sweat night | fever lore
and it ain't gonna go smooth now, Madora

field songs | the mission | flowing through my vision
but, I ain't gonna see you no more

silent precision creepin' through Master's kitchen
no, it ain't gonna go smooth, Madora

so muddled the melody
border states of malady
ground water running clean
skimming cream off dream
and I'll get home

law made property | auction | rapture | shatter plate
and I ain't gonna see you no more

fought me | can't see | no knock warrant | cold slate
and it ain't gonna go smooth now, Madora

was a no-name puppeteer
rain fell like overseer
keyholes to fantasy
up quiet in the canopy

and I'll keep on

but, I ain't gonna see you no more, Madora
was never gonna go right this time

56. This Love

No crooked-ass coal smokestack mornings. No limestone fortress orchid apparitions. No prenatal election night insomnia. No palm wine or border cages. Ain't no flimsy minarets to this love.

And I know it's whatcha thinking of, how we never much matter to some: slick street wonders, work/service/coin, chattel runs.

But, our people dreamed us, dreamed us for the crux of this world. Never leaked us (hair, teeth, gums) leaked us of their stars. So, we drink them by verse lines. Thousandth crane. Troubles of soul. Chrysalis of mind.

We got cold chasing the liquid gold. And if the baby's sold, don't drain the river, *hold*. Because we need you more than liquor store, than hit the floor, than chords, Fords, waterboards, than freedom gourds could ever show.

Crayon candle airbrush street altar. Blood dawn prison ribbon incisions. Cut cane sorrow. Grave songs. Saltwater freefall. Menthols. Forever, no flimsy minarets to this love.

57. Why Didn't It Rain?

when she asks if the man making masters is real
if the storm made of masters is real, you say:

> hot watch night breeze
> torn tender things
> no-knock dreams
> what it means | busted seams | sugar cane
> why didn't it rain?

> the song careens
> the stolen kings
> the body steams
> what it means | twisted trees | pretty stains
> why didn't it rain?

> let no bone white light
> no concrete sling
> no perfume cream
> no noosed moonbeam turn our eyes away
> why didn't it rain?

> sweet baby girl, why didn't it rain?
> rain on you | fresh taro | free sparrow
> was a crooked game
> no one heard the birds we love
> all the pills I named
> so we took it underground and now
> why didn't it rain?

made to run | black mold | Black minds won't be explained
in this creeping rain
and the pills I'd blame
and the demons you'll slay for play
why didn't it rain?
why didn't it rain?

their lizard scales
shorn iron fangs
stomach pangs
chain gangs | klux klans | book bans | our names
why didn't it rain?

and heirloom hair
the people sang
that midnight bang
was just too much for one single vein
why didn't it rain?

from nightmare sails
to framed life spans
in strange lands
fangs | clangs | a trance | where we'll feel no pain
why didn't it rain?

sweet baby girl, why didn't it rain?
rain for you | harm's arrow | life's marrow
right down the drain
with the slurs they flung
and the kids they maimed
to the heavens we did proclaim aloud

why didn't it rain?
gotta run | sold | no doors | higher planes
in this creeping rain
and the ills we'd gain
was the truth of pain | *mute sound*
why didn't it rain?
why didn't it rain?

yes, the man making masters is real, my love
and the storm made of masters is real, my love

yes, the man making masters is real, my love
and the storm made of masters is real, my love
but we be forged of doves

why didn't it rain?
rain on you | was narrow | too narrow
nothing ends the same
not a bell unrung
not a curve made straight
so we circle the burial mound and now
why didn't it rain?
final fold | blown out | 1,000 cranes
in this creeping rain
and we swerved in vain
but the truth so plain | to clay
why didn't it rain?
why didn't it rain?

58. Last Rites

we leave you here with a song
keep a place for us

        ivory totem, sharpened bone
        cowries for currency
        slaughtered hog
        all the song
        keep a place for us

you, bundled newborn baby
we, your people singing
keep a place for us

        leaving just the way we came
        but short one body
        and one song

            we be runnin' runnin' runnin' runnin' runnin'

notes & acknowledgements

Many thanks to the editors and staff of the following publications in which early versions of these poems have appeared:

Juked: "Lord's Prayer, 1910," "This Trembling"
Jubilat: "Huck"
Fourteen Hills: The SFSU Review: "Indian Removal act of 1830"
Bayou Magazine: "Coke Bottle Blues"
Journal of the Plague Year: "Eulogy"
Cagibi: "Oath"
The Harvard Advocate: "John Brown"
Poetry Magazine: "13th Amendment," "Miranda/Point 8"

...

"The Widow Versus the Devil—Huck Runs for Cover" (#5) includes lyrics from the traditional African American hymn, "He's Sweet, I Know."

"Untitled" (#8 and those that follow) is after the Indian Removal Act of 1830.

"Eulogy" (#18 and those that follow) is after the Eulogy Delivered by Ossie Davis at the Funeral of Malcolm X, Feb. 27, 1965.

"Some Nerve" (#19) references the jazz standard, "You Don't Know What Love Is."

"Balm in Gilead" (#23) is after the traditional African American spiritual, "There is a Balm in Gilead" and the corresponding footnote is after the Maya Angelou poem, "Not Long Ago."

"John Brown" (#33) is after Brown's final speech, "Address of John Brown to the Virginia Court, 1859."

"Oath" (#39) is after the U.S. Presidential Oath of Office.

"Golden Eyes" (#41) is inspired by the short story, "Dark They Were, and Golden-Eyed" by Ray Bradbury.

"The Keys" (#48) includes a line from the Outkast song, "SpottieOttieDopaliscious."

"Fugue" (#51) is after two poems: "Death Fugue" by Paul Celan and "sorrow song" by Lucille Clifton.

The "13th Amendment" sequence (#54) contains edited images originally obtained from the Open Access Digital Archive of the Collection of the Smithsonian National Museum of African American History and Culture (titled: Broadside advertising "Valuable Slaves at Auction" in New Orleans (2014.63.16)).

Thank you, God, for getting me over.

Thank you, Diane Goettel & the whole Black Lawrence Press staff for taking a chance on this book.

Thank you, Michaela Mullin, Lorraine Lupo, and Youssef Alaoui for your encouragement, feedback and support.

Thank you to my amazing family: Mom, Dad, Jen, Dallas, Matty, and Mason.

Thank you to my brilliant and loving wife, Alivia.

Keith Donnell Jr. is a Philly born poet, writer, and book editor. He is the author of *The Move* (Nomadic Press, 2021) and his work has been published in numerous journals and anthologies. He currently resides in Seaside, California.